W9-AFS-672

NEW HAMPSHIRE

Julie M

VISIT US AT
www.abdopublishing.com

Published by ABDO Publishing Company, PO Box 398166, Minneapolis, MN 55439.

Printed in the United States of America, North Mankato, Minnesota.
042012
092012

♻ PRINTED ON RECYCLED PAPER

Coordinating Series Editor: Rochelle Baltzer
Editor: Sarah Tieck
Contributing Editors: Megan M. Gunderson, BreAnn Rumsch, Marcia Zappa
Graphic Design: Adam Craven
Cover Photograph: *iStockphoto*: ©iStockphoto.com/ScottOrr.
Interior Photographs/Illustrations: *AP Photo*: Jim Cole (p. 27), NASA (p. 25), NASA, HO (p. 25), North Wind Picture Archives via AP Images (pp. 13, 23); *Getty Images*: Rick Bouthiette (p. 19), Richard Cummins (p. 27), Stock Montage (p. 13); *iStockphoto*: ©iStockphoto.com/aimintang (p. 17), ©iStockphoto.com/SteveByland (p. 30), ©iStockphoto.com/MikeCherim (p. 30), ©iStockphoto.com/coleong (p. 26), ©iStockphoto.com/katatonia82 (p. 30), ©iStockphoto.com/DougLemke (p. 29), ©iStockphoto.com/Mshake (p. 21), ©iStockphoto.com/DenisTangneyJr (pp. 9, 11, 26); *Shutterstock*: drewthehobbit (p. 27), Jeffrey M. Frank (p. 9), Eric Full (p. 5), Philip Lange (p. 30).

All population figures taken from the 2010 US census.

Library of Congress Cataloging-in-Publication Data

Murray, Julie, 1969-
  New Hampshire / Julie Murray.
    p. cm. -- (Explore the United States)
  ISBN 978-1-61783-367-0
  1. New Hampshire--Juvenile literature. I. Title.
  F34.3.M87 2013
  974.2--dc23
                        2012010553

Contents

ONE NATION

The United States is a **diverse** country. It has farmland, cities, coasts, and mountains. Its people come from many different backgrounds. And, its history covers more than 200 years.

Today the country includes 50 states. New Hampshire is one of these states. Let's learn more about this state and its story!

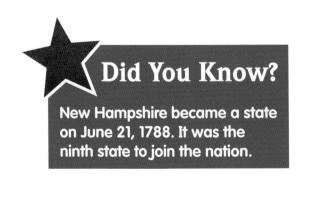

Did You Know?

New Hampshire became a state on June 21, 1788. It was the ninth state to join the nation.

Much of New Hampshire is covered in thick forests.

New Hampshire Up Close

The United States has four main **regions**. New Hampshire is in the Northeast.

New Hampshire has three states on its borders. Massachusetts is south. Vermont is west and Maine is east. The country of Canada is north. And, the Atlantic Ocean is southeast.

New Hampshire is a small state. Its total area is 9,280 square miles (24,035 sq km). About 1.3 million people live there.

Did You Know?

Washington DC is the US capital city. Puerto Rico is a US commonwealth. This means it is governed by its own people.

REGIONS OF THE UNITED STATES

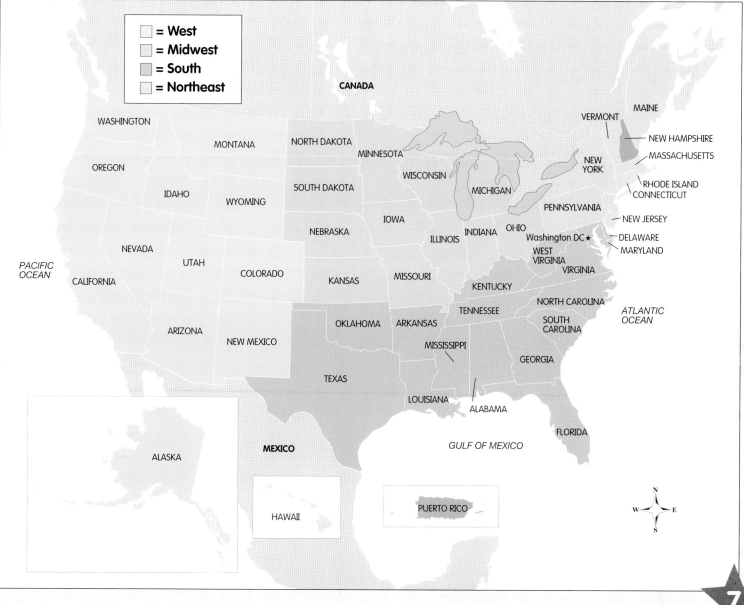

= West
= Midwest
= South
= Northeast

CANADA

WASHINGTON
MONTANA
NORTH DAKOTA
MINNESOTA
VERMONT
MAINE
NEW HAMPSHIRE
OREGON
MASSACHUSETTS
IDAHO
WYOMING
SOUTH DAKOTA
WISCONSIN
MICHIGAN
NEW YORK
RHODE ISLAND
CONNECTICUT
IOWA
PENNSYLVANIA
NEW JERSEY
NEVADA
UTAH
NEBRASKA
ILLINOIS
INDIANA
OHIO
Washington DC ★
DELAWARE
MARYLAND
WEST VIRGINIA
VIRGINIA
PACIFIC OCEAN
CALIFORNIA
COLORADO
KANSAS
MISSOURI
KENTUCKY
NORTH CAROLINA
ATLANTIC OCEAN
TENNESSEE
ARIZONA
NEW MEXICO
OKLAHOMA
ARKANSAS
SOUTH CAROLINA
MISSISSIPPI
GEORGIA
TEXAS
LOUISIANA
ALABAMA
FLORIDA
ALASKA
MEXICO
GULF OF MEXICO
HAWAII
PUERTO RICO

N
W E
S

7

IMPORTANT CITIES

Concord is New Hampshire's **capital**. It is also the state's third-largest city, with 42,695 people. This city's history dates to the 1720s. It has a historic downtown and Main Street.

Manchester is the largest city in the state. It is home to 109,565 people. It is known for its strong business community.

8

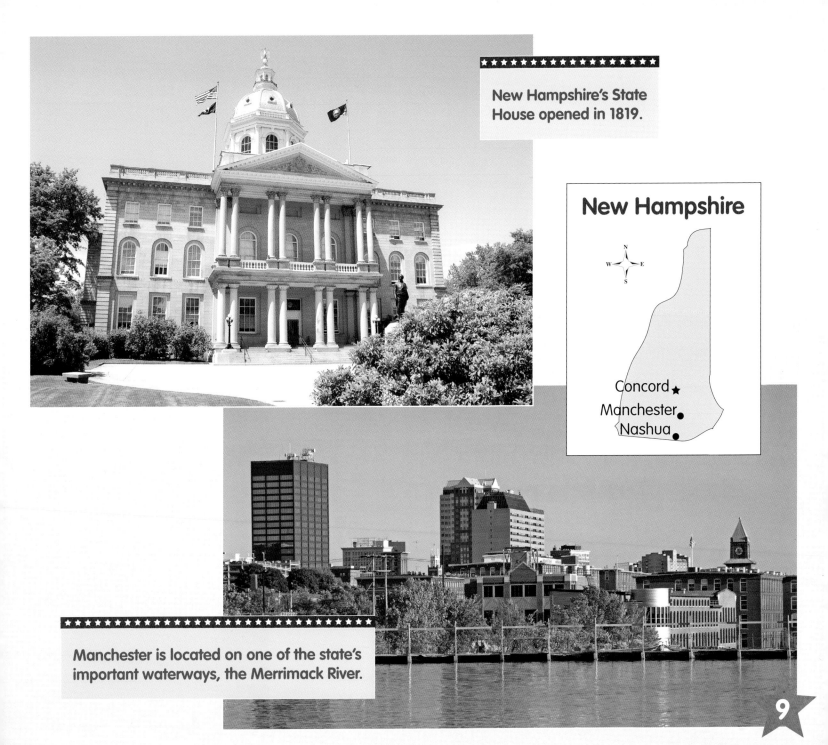

New Hampshire's State House opened in 1819.

New Hampshire

Concord ★
Manchester ●
Nashua ●

Manchester is located on one of the state's important waterways, the Merrimack River.

9

Nashua (NA-shuh-wuh) is New Hampshire's second-largest city. It is home to 86,494 people. This city is close to the state of Massachusetts. It is near Silver Lake State Park. People swim and picnic there.

Nashua was settled around 1660.
It has many historic buildings.

11

New Hampshire in History

New Hampshire's history includes settlers and war. New Hampshire began as an English colony in the 1600s. The first settlers arrived in 1623.

In the 1700s, colonists wanted to be part of a new country. So, they fought in the **Revolutionary War** and formed the United States. In 1788, New Hampshire became the ninth state.

Did You Know?

Native Americans lived in present-day New Hampshire for thousands of years before the colony formed.

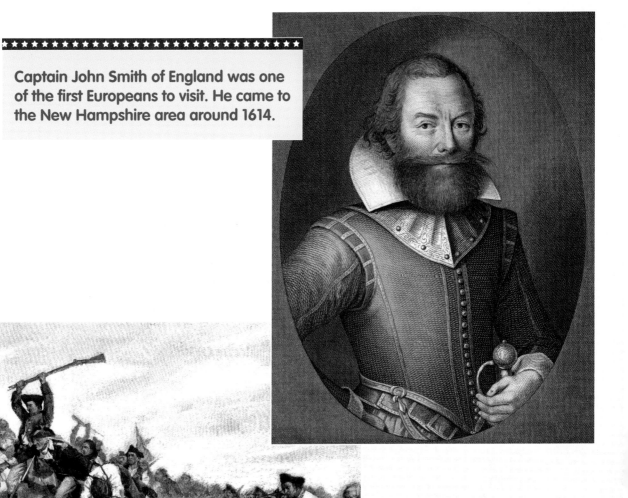

Captain John Smith of England was one of the first Europeans to visit. He came to the New Hampshire area around 1614.

Many men from New Hampshire fought and died in the Revolutionary War.

Timeline

1833

The Peterborough Public Library was established. It was one of the first in the United States.

1853

Franklin Pierce of Hillsborough became the fourteenth US president.

Concord became New Hampshire's **capital**.

1808

The **American Civil War** began. New Hampshire fought for the Northern states.

1861

1800s

1944

New Hampshire hosted the Bretton Woods Conference. The World Bank was founded at this important event.

1997

Jeanne Shaheen became New Hampshire's first female governor.

2012

New Hampshire held the nation's first US presidential **primary** of the year. This is one of the first major voting steps in choosing a president.

1900s

2000s

Alan B. Shepard Jr. of East Derry became the first American in space.

1961

The Old Man of the Mountain broke off and fell to the ground. This rock formation was one of the state's famous landmarks.

2003

ACROSS THE LAND

New Hampshire has hills, forests, lakes, and rivers. The White Mountains cover part of the state. The Connecticut and Merrimack Rivers flow through New Hampshire. Also, part of the state borders the Atlantic Ocean.

Many types of animals make their homes in New Hampshire. These include moose, white-tailed deer, and beavers.

Did You Know?

In July, the average temperature in New Hampshire is 68°F (20°C). In January, it is 19°F (-7°C).

Lake Winnipesaukee is the largest lake in the state.

Earning a Living

New Hampshire has many important businesses. Some people have jobs helping visitors to the state. Others work in manufacturing jobs making electronics and paper. People in the state also work in finance, education, and health care.

New Hampshire has many natural **resources**. Mines produce sand, gravel, and **granite**. Farms provide apples, dairy products, cattle, and hay.

Lobsters and fish are caught off of New Hampshire's coast.

Natural Wonder

The White Mountains are in northern New Hampshire. Their most famous area is called the Presidential Range. Eight of its peaks are named after US presidents.

Mount Washington is the most famous mountain peak in the range. It is known for having wild weather. In April 1934, the wind speed there was recorded at 231 miles (372 km) per hour. That was a world record for more than 75 years!

Mount Washington is the highest point in New Hampshire. It stands 6,288 feet (1,917 m) tall!

HOMETOWN HEROES

Many famous people are from New Hampshire. Franklin Pierce was born in Hillsborough in 1804. He was the fourteenth US president. Pierce served from 1853 to 1857. During this time, the country faced disagreements that led to the **American Civil War**.

Did You Know?

Pierce is the only US president from New Hampshire.

When Pierce was president,
the United States was growing.
People were moving west.

23

Astronaut Alan B. Shepard Jr. was born in East Derry in 1923. On May 5, 1961, he became the first American to travel in space.

Christa McAuliffe was born in 1948 in Boston, Massachusetts. She later worked as a teacher in Concord. McAuliffe was chosen as the first teacher and non-astronaut to go into space. In 1986, she boarded the space shuttle *Challenger*. Sadly, it exploded after liftoff. McAuliffe and the other astronauts died.

Shepard was 37 when he traveled to space on the *Freedom 7*.

McAuliffe had planned to teach lessons from space.

Tour Book

Do you want to go to New Hampshire? If you visit the state, here are some places to go and things to do!

★ Play

Ski in New Hampshire's mountains in the winter. In the summer, you can ride on many of the ski lifts for a great view!

★ Discover

Walk the grounds of Dartmouth College in Hanover. This well-known school was founded in 1769.

★ Remember

Check out the Museum of New Hampshire History in Concord. Exhibits explore important moments in the state's past.

★ Explore

Visit the White Mountain National Forest. Many people like to hike its trails.

★ See

Spend the day at the McAuliffe-Shepard Discovery Center in Concord. There, you can visit a planetarium and learn about space travel.

A GREAT STATE

The story of New Hampshire is important to the United States. The people and places that make up this state offer something special to the country. Together with all the states, New Hampshire helps make the United States great.

New Hampshire has only 18 miles (29 km) of coastline. Much of it is rugged and rocky.

Fast Facts

Date of Statehood:
June 21, 1788

Population (rank):
1,316,470
(42nd most-populated state)

Total Area (rank):
9,280 square miles
(44th largest state)

Motto:
"Live Free or Die"

Nickname:
Granite State

State Capital:
Concord

Flag:

Flower: Purple Lilac

Postal Abbreviation:
NH

Tree: White Birch

Bird: Purple Finch

Important Words

American Civil War the war between the Northern and Southern states from 1861 to 1865.

astronaut a person who is trained for space travel.

capital a city where government leaders meet.

diverse made up of things that are different from each other.

granite a type of very hard rock often used for building.

primary an election before the main election in which members of the same political party run against each other. Voters choose candidates to run in the main election.

region a large part of a country that is different from other parts.

resource a supply of something useful or valued.

Revolutionary War a war fought between England and the North American colonies from 1775 to 1783.

Web Sites

To learn more about New Hampshire, visit ABDO Publishing Company online. Web sites about New Hampshire are featured on our Book Links page. These links are routinely monitored and updated to provide the most current information available.

www.abdopublishing.com

Index